SILENT SUFFOCATION

The Walter Dumas Story

Based On A True Story

For contact information:
World Movement Publishing LLC
407 N. Pacific Coast Highway, Suite 1064
Redondo Beach, CA 90277
info@worldmovement.com
website: www.worldmovement.com

ISBN 13: 978-0-9828768-8-6
Library of Congress Control Number: 2023951022

World Movement Publishing LLC books may be purchased for educational, business, or sales promotional use.
For information, please contact:
World Movement Publishing LLC
407 N. Pacific Coast Highway, Suite 1064
Redondo Beach, CA 90277
info@worldmovement.com
website: www.worldmovement.com

Cover design by Djhn

Contents

· ·●· ·

Dedication

· ·●· ·

First and foremost, I dedicate this book to Ronnie (Brother Adams), who is family to me and my friend. Through my ups and downs, who has stuck by me throughout the years, created an excellent documentary on my life (Surviving the O.K. Boys Ranch: The Walter Dumas Story). I thank you and appreciate you.

To the World Movement Publishing LLC team, Lamont Patterson, CEO, Olivia Shannon, my publisher, and Rebecca Mahan, my publicist. I also thank you and appreciate you for helping me tell my life story (Silent Suffocation: The Walter Dumas Story), a very horrific and painful time in my life.

And last but certainly not least, my wife, Shelly, has stuck by me through all these painful, hurtful moments I have endured in the last few years of my life. I love you and appreciate you.

In closing, I pray that God grants success to this book and that it may touch lives help others who are struggling from abuse and so they can, like me, move forward and heal.

Amen.

Walter Dumas

··●··

The beginning

1970s to 1980

··●··

My childhood was spotty at best. I don't believe I had a childhood because I was passed around from place to place, home to home, aunts, uncles, grandparents, and strangers. I didn't have time to breathe and be a child because my childhood was abusive, dysfunctional, and neglectful. I was born Walter Lee Dumas on November 13, 1972, in the elevator at the University of Washington Hospital on the 11th floor. My mother was in my life from when I was born to age six or seven. I barely saw my dad because he was in and out of our lives and very abusive, especially to my mother. He beat her cold days on in, and I believe it triggered her to hate men, and it came off on us kids, my brother Anthony Dumas and sister Ramona Dumas. You did something stupid or behaved badly; she beat us with whatever she had on hand: irons, extension cords, brushes, sticks, etc. The beatings were so bad because she aimed at whatever: our backs, our privates, our heads, and so on. It was excruciating what I experienced. My mother was old school like my grandparents, and their idea of discipline was to beat you into submission, to get you to listen and understand.

I guess that comes from where they were born and raised: Natchez, Mississippi. My mother was born on an old cotton plantation on January 19, 1952. Whatever her experiences and things she went through were sometimes horrific, we had to deal with it too. I don't know much about my family history, only where my mother was from January 1952, my father Walter Lee Dumas Jr., June 14, 1941, my mom Natchez, Mississippi, and my father from Hughes, Arkansas. How and why, they ended up in Seattle, Washington, is a mystery to me and my uncles and grandparents, spotty like my childhood before age 8, when I would have entered the foster care system. I know my mom met my dad at Monroe Prison Farm, Monroe, Washington, when she was 18, and he married her at 19. And that is the extent of what I know about my childhood between birth and age 6 or 7. It was a lot of trauma experienced, physical, emotional, and sexual abuse, plus neglect I went through and caused me to run away. So much so that the Seattle, Washington, police got tired of taking me back and forth to my mom. At that time, I suffered a lot of depression, an x i e t y, and fears in my childhood. I have two other siblings, stepbrothers Freddy and Jerome Jones, when my mom married their dad, Freddy Jones Jr., in 1979. She favored them over me and my brother and sister, Ramona and Anthony Dumas, so more often than not, I was sad and hurt and had resentment towards them, which brought me a great deal of pain and caused me to run away even more. Especially when my mom wasn't around, often in the street, chasing men doing her own thing. So, as children, there was often no food in the home to eat, no furniture to sit on, or beds to sleep in. This was my daily life. On top of seeing and experiencing in my family divorce, alcoholism, drug abuse, sexual molestation, and violence, that's truly rough for a child to see and experience. Especially with my father, who was in and out of our lives and was psychotic and crazy, abused my mother constantly, and hurt us sometimes. To this day, there are pictures of us floating around, including my mom, tied up in the woods, and my father was a hunter, standing by with bags full of bloody dead rabbits. I don't know if that was a warning or what, but until this day, I believe my father was going to murder us. He was straight crazy. And when I say my father was straight crazy, there was one occasion when I remember my father kicked my grandparents' door in and started beating on my mom. My grandfather chased my father down the street with a gun to kill him. I, a young thing, ran after him, crying and saying to my grandfather, "Please don't kill my father."

It was tough and painful to remember some of this, but it's a fact, and it did happen. That's sad and traumatizing because I believe childhood is supposed to be the happiest time in a person's life. You constantly learn something new when you don't have any care, good parents, a stable home, meals, friends, and playgrounds to play in. But that was not the case for me. My childhood is a living horror story, a cruel world filled with hurt, emotional damage, and uncertainty. And so, my final time to escape from home, from my daily abuse, I didn't look back at that time—Department of Social and Health Services (age 8, the sad life). I believe I was eight years old or so, tired, scared, and just wanted to feel safe. So, I ran away and fell asleep on a Seattle, Washington, park bench, where the police found me and took me to the Department of Social and Health Services. That's when everything started to go downhill for me. When they called my mom, she came, and I refused to go home with her. They tried, but I went crazy, acting up, crying, and throwing stuff everywhere until they restrained me. They told my mom she would have to go to court, so they kept me and placed me in a receiving home (receiving homes are temporary living situations). I bounced around from place to place, different families, no happy times, and I was physically, sexually, and emotionally abused in some homes. Eventually, over months, I returned to my mom, but my behaviors and moods got worse because of the continued beatings from my mom. I developed haphephobia, the fear of being touched. Every noise and quick movement frightened me and drove me to an insane set of moods.

A Childhood Lost: A Life Poem by Walter Dumas

To endure and to live.
My childhood and my innocence I had to give.
With no hope and no faith, only tragedy and pain.
Consumed by my fear, my sadness comes down like
      a stormy rain.
Breaking me down to my knees,
to suffer parental neglect, and to be beat, tortured,
      and raped by life.
Digging into me, mind, body, and soul, both emotionally
      and physically, like a sharp edge of a knife.
This was my childhood: no fun times, no playgrounds, no
      Smiles or laughter, just passed around like a raggedy
      bus ticket at every cost. This was life for me,
      "a childhood lost.".

Bible verse: 1 Corinthians 13:4-8, "abuse is impatient abuse is unkind. It is envious, it boasts, it is proud. It dishonors others; it is self-seeking; it is easily angered; it keeps a record of wrongs. Abuse delights in evil, but it's miserable with the truth. It never protects, never perseveres, abuse always fails..." my mother got tired of me, but what she didn't understand and was doing to me emotionally and physically took a heavy toll on me. In the early '80s, the Department of Social Health Service assigned me a case worker, so they came and took me out of the home. It would be one of the last times I would return home when placed at the Seattle Children's Hospital Behavioral Medicine Unit in Seattle, Washington. This place would become my home for the next 11 months, where I became more angry, resentful, and bitter. So, during those months, I tried running away, but that place you're locked in. So I fought with staff, tore things up, and experienced being put in restraints, sometimes in a straitjacket, and loaded with Ritalin by administrator staff.

Over time, I became more compliant that the Juvenile Court of Seattle, Washington, decided to place me in the foster care system, a trash dump for children. And this started my path into the foster care system. So, since there were no beds, I was placed back in receiving homes and placed with various families. You didn't know where you would live or who with whom. Someone told me to pack my bags. I'm moving, which happens constantly, moving me many times in the middle of the night. It was simply exhausting to go through this process. I developed even more emotional behavioral problems and difficult, painful, hurtful, and challenging behaviors. Especially being a person of color, I went through hell once I reached the foster care system after I spent so much time in receiving homes and mental institutions. It's just in my eyes that it got worse because I never got the best of nothing, and it never was a safe, loving, and inclusive environment that would allow me to have anything I could call home. It didn't exist, and there was no support or no care. Personally, in Seattle, Washington, and various places, the foster care system was designed to break you, hurt you, forget about you, and leave you lost in their system. The money they gave the foster care parents to care for me, and you will hear a lot they spent on themselves and their families. So, I didn't get the best food or nutrition I needed. They bought my clothes from secondhand stores like the Salvation Army. Hand me down rags. I called them back at that time. And it got me picked on, bullied, and called many racist names, n*****, negro, foster care rat, trash, big lips, nappy-headed bastard, just to name a few. And so, I acted out more and more and once again ran away. And the more I ran, the further out they tried to place me as punishment for my actions. And so, my caseworker can once again place me somewhere else. I was so angry and started arguing with him because I felt like he didn't care or understand, as a child, what I was going through. As he drove me to a new placement and foster home, I grabbed the steering wheel and tried killing us both. So, he pulled over, and we fought and argued for a few minutes. Eventually, I calmed down so he could take me where he had to, but I was miserable, unhappy, and full of tears.

Uncertain if this place was better than the last. Trust me, it was not. And it was during this time in the 1980s my mother would come back into the picture now and then because it was juvenile court mandated. But it never worked out. The judge and case workers looked at my mom as an uneducated, unintelligent, crazy black woman who couldn't handle or care for her children, based on investigation into the home and even police reports. So, I remained with the foster care system I was in till the next court date, which was mandatory for my mom to make decisions and to figure out what to do with me. But when that time came months later, my mom didn't show up to court, and they couldn't reach her by phone. They tried other relatives, but they didn't want to take me, as they considered me to have too many behavioral issues and would be a bad influence on their children (my cousins) and wouldn't feel safe. The judge had no choice but to permanently award me to the state of Washington and revoke my mother's parental rights. That devastated me and broke me down so badly. To this day, I have never forgiven my mother. And so I went back to the foster home I was in temporarily and then moved to a group home in Richmond Beach, Washington, the Distad family group home. I will experience, one of the few times, a group home with other boys.

Two parents and their children lived upstairs, and six or seven of us boys lived downstairs with on-call staff. I found the home and everything in it strange. One, because it was Mormon-like, we had to attend church seven days a week, school mandatory, and Bible study readings at night. I had several behavioral issues and learning problems. I couldn't cope with this type of life. I did okay for the first few months there, but once again, I started acting up in school and tried running away. I was taken back to the group home and beaten by Mr. Distad in his office with a hard wooden paddle. I think he enjoyed it. It hurt like hell. I experienced this a few times, and I got sick and tired of it and once again ran away. I took a few boys with me this time, and we broke into homes, stole stuff, and for the first-time experienced drinking alcohol, but I wouldn't say I liked it. We were caught, had to go to juvenile children's court, and then sent back to Distads. As I was the one who started this mess, the Distads decided I was too much to handle, too many behavioral issues, and told me I would have to leave. So, they contacted my caseworker, who said to give them time, they would have to come up with a replacement. I begged to stay, but the Distads packed my bags a few weeks later. And I was sent back to a receiving home temporarily until they could find a more permanent solution.

·•·

Ruth Dykeman Children's Center:

Formerly Called "The Loft"

1982-1983

·•·

Somewhere in there, I left the receiving home and was told by my caseworker that they had found me a more permanent solution, and they hoped this would work out this time. So, they sent me to Burien, Washington, to a place formally called "The Loft," now called the "Ruth Dykeman Children's Center." I remember it very well because it was no group home. My caseworker said it was a group home by a lake, and I would like it. It turns out not to be the case. Unknown to me, this horrible place was a children's behavioral center. Also unbeknownst to me, but in later years, I would find out this place was a 15-bed lakeside cottage supervised by staff members with nurses and psychologists who were on call for behavioral, emotional, and mental health needs. So, when the caseworker pulled up, I was happy, knowing there was a lake, but I was misled as I had often been in my life. There was staff waiting when I got there. They took my bags, I hugged my caseworker goodbye, and he handed my files over. This was strange to me. My caseworker was not coming in, so I cried and was told everything would be all right. The staff led me through a door, which I heard a click and locked behind me. I was startled, so I tried to go back through the door, but the door wouldn't open. They took me to the nurses' station, where staff and a supervisor assessed me, assigned me a room, and gave me their type of clothes to wear (sweatshirts and slippers). They took my shoes and belongings. So, I lived at the Ruth Dykeman Children's Center for months, worsening my behavior. I fought with staff constantly, put in restraints, and given medications daily like Ritalin, Wellbutrin, Lexapro, and other shit I can't name.

What the fuck? I mean, damn. I was doped up half the time. I didn't know if I was coming or going. It was a straight fucking nightmare, to say the least. This damn sure was no group home, and I endured this for several months, just a slave to the system slowly destroying my childhood.

Finally, one day, I was assigned a new caseworker and staff from Olympia Kiwanis Boys Ranch (O.K. Boys Ranch) from Olympia, Washington, who would come every few weeks to assess me. Finally, a determination was made that I would be a perfect case (mind you, back in those motherfucking days, sonsofbitches, thought of you as a case, a tracking number, not a child, not a human being, but less than, like trash hauled off to the dump) for a long-term permanent placement. My brother, Anthony Dumas, came to live at the Ruth Dykeman Children's Center, and that was my only sense of family. But the O.K. Boys Ranch staff said they couldn't take both of us; only one of us, the older one, was me. Mind you, it was like selecting the best stock cow, if you will, for their farm. That was heartbreaking and devastating. So, the time I have, I spent with my brother until a few weeks later. The caseworker came and took me to Olympia, Washington, and even brought my brother along for the ride as comfort, as I was terrified, sad, and uncertain about where I was going and what would happen to me (mind you, having been placed so much in so many places, I felt like branded cattle at an auction). The ride to Olympia, Washington, from Burien, Washington, was long. I've never been that far away from Seattle,

Washington, and I remember feeling overwhelmed and nervous, going to a strange place I had never been. I was around ten and a half years old when I arrived at the O.K. Boys Ranch.

·· • ···

1983 "Olympia Kiwanis Boys Ranch"

And the Destruction of My Childhood

·· • ···

Olympia Kiwanis " O.K. Boys Ranch," a so-called group home, resided in eastern Olympia, Washington. I was shocked when we arrived at the O.K. Boys Ranch in the afternoon. I mean totally fucking shocked because this was no ranch at all that I was led to believe where I was going to live. Even my caseworker at the time was dumbfounded. There were no horses, cows, chickens, pigs, fenced-in fences, barns, farm hands, or farm machinery. The Olympia Kiwanis O.K. Boys Ranch was a broken-down-looking tract home, an oversized-looking trailer park in the eastern part of Olympia, Washington, founded in 1971. A director ran it, Thomas van Woerdan, who had a staff of Collette Queener, assistant director, and former nun who lived in the house along with counselor and staff Laura Rambo Russell and some on-call staff who temporarily lived upstairs on the property, plus a psychotherapist who would come weekly. This was no ordinary group home; it was something else entirely.

There was nothing family about it at all. When I arrived, Thomas van Woerdan, the director, greeted me. He was a strange-looking man with pale, freckled skin, carrot-top red hair, a trim mustache, scary devilish light blue eyes, a tie, and a sweater, very strange. I also was met by the on-call psychotherapist, a black woman. She was okay. We toured the entire property. Upstairs, the downstairs, the TV room, the offices, the backyard, the outside office. I met a few boys and the cook, Mrs. Gwen, a strange German lady I would come to hate. I remembered she always cooked the same shit, strange pasta dishes, or if you were bad, she fed you scraps, slop, mess, or shit order for prisons.

And so, I was given a set of rules, plus put on a level system. Its purpose was to control you. Level one, you don't get shit. No freedom, no outings, no nothing. The higher the level, the more freedom you get, rewards, etc." This was supposed to be a family group home, but it was run like one of those behavioral centers or mental health institutions, a psychiatric hospital. Definitely not Mom and Pop's comfy feel, but cold, dark, and mysterious.

Anyway, it was time for my caseworker and my brother to leave. That was very hard on me, but it still impacts me today because I won't see my brother again for years. I hugged the caseworker and then my brother, who I cried with. They had to pry us apart. To me, as they were leaving. I tried running after them, but Ranch staff and the psychotherapist pulled me back. I was placed in my assigned room to calm down. Later, I was allowed to go downstairs to watch TV in the TV room. This was a strange room, too. We have a locked door, rugged benches for seating, a weird-looking TV, and a small Library plexiglass window so the staff can always look in on us. Very 70's, trippy place, to say the least. After that, I was given towels, soap, and a toothbrush and led to the bathroom upstairs for a shower before dinner. The bathroom was scary as shit, I mean truly scary. This was no ordinary family bathroom, a comfortable, cozy bathroom. This was a huge, long, institutional white bathroom with toilet stalls, no doors and open shower units, no privacy, think prison bathroom. After my shower, I went downstairs for dinner, met with the rest of the boys, Miss Gwen, the cook, assistant director Collette, staff counselor Laura Rambo Russell, and that was that. By 8:00

p.m., it was time for bed, and I was exhausted after that long drive to get here. My room was not a happy place. The room was a strange blue, with wood fixtures, wood paneling, and strange wallpaper, and my bed was inside a wooden box with storage underneath.

Very 1970s, to say the least. I closed my eyes to go to sleep, only to be woken up by older boys, told to be quiet. That was midnight, mind you, and led downstairs and outside to the backyard. As a newcomer to the boys' Ranch, everything seemed normal, so I thought. Two of the older boys grabbed me and stuck a sock in my mouth, and then I was tied to the basketball pole, rope around my neck, and my hands tied. I was so fucking terrified of what was going to happen to me, and a boy told me that I was a fish, a newcomer, and this was "Initiation Night" for new fish. So, I had piss and shit thrown on me and beaten with hard soap in long socks. Crying and traumatized, the older boys said, "Welcome to the O.K. Boys Ranch," and let me go with a stern warning, "Don't say anything to staff or the other boys." But things will get much worse. Mind you, I had suffered ongoing physical, sexual, mental, and emotional abuse from my earlier childhood and being out of numerous foster homes, receiving homes, and group homes, to name a few places, so I didn't say anything, not even to school staff.

The next day, I started school at Nisqually Middle School, 8100 Steilacoom Road Southeast, Lacey, Washington, 98503. For the first few months, everything was okay. Then, I started getting bullied daily by a bully. Slammed into the lockers, beat up. I tried fighting back but to no avail. Sometimes, I even starved in school because he'd steal my lunches. So, I developed a lot of anger, which reflected back at the Boys Ranch. And I constantly fought with ranch staff, especially director Thomas van Woerdan. He always put me in a corner as punishment for hours; my legs used to hurt. From this, I fought with Laura Rambo Russell, another Ranch staffer who used to do strange shit to me, weird, freaky bitch. Also, another staffer, Collette Queener, used to make me rub her feet and lay beside her bed as punishment. That was fucking strange to me. She also hit me with sticks. As she was a former nun, this is why I fucking hate churches. Motherfuckers do strange shit to you, especially in preaching, and she used to restrain me as further punishment as well.

As I said, we had on-call staff and two staff members living upstairs. They were changing constantly, one in particular, 400 lb—Rod Daly, who came to live at the Ranch. I fought with him, too. Fucker was huge, mind you. I was a short, skinny kid, about 11 years old, by the time of my birthday, and maybe 4'11 or so. His ideal punishment was to kick me in my back or my hips and sit on me. It's why my back and my hips are messed up today. A year into this, living at The Boys Ranch, I was fighting with the boys constantly and getting into trouble at school, so I always stayed at the bottom of the level system at the Ranch. Never to take trips or have freedom. Punishment at the Ranch varied.

One night I was picking up cigarette butts, plus trash, and staff followed behind me in their car or ranch van. And another time, I was taken to Thomas van Woerdan's office, door shut, and beaten with a wooden paddle till my ass, back, and legs were sore, red, and blistered. I tell you, it was hard living in this horrific place. I tried starving myself; it felt like Mrs. Gwen was trying to poison me with her food. I used to throw that sloppy shit up against the wall, breaking dishes in the process. Another time, I tried killing myself, I wish I had, and ended up with a paid outpatient therapist. Every time I came to her office, she'd give me coffee so I could ease up and talk. The coffee was strange to me and made me drowsy and sleepy. Unknown to me, and I will find out years later, this particular therapist was hired by O.K. Boys Ranch, not by the state of Washington. Everything said in that office, she was going back and telling Director Thomas van Woerdan, and we get punished, or he will put the older boys on us. It was like a fucking wild jungle living at The Boys Ranch. The older boys and staff were the lions, and the younger boys were the zebras, the prey, and we were constantly preyed on by these predators, especially David, who came to live with us. I remember him well because he was a special needs kid with many problems. As much was done to me, David got it ten times worse. I witnessed his rape in the upstairs bathroom, that was heartbreaking. They forced me to watch as a reminder of what could happen to me. For me, my rapes started almost a year into living at The Boys Ranch. They made me suck dicks, pushed my head down into the toilets constantly while anally raping me from behind. This happened on a few occasions, especially in my bedroom. I was raped with the door shut. Punched and kicked in my back, slapped in the face always, kicked in my face, some teeth cracked, forced to watch orgies going on, forced to watch younger boys get raped sometimes daily. I tell you, I truly went through some fucking shit.

One night, as a boy finished raping me, I waited until everybody slept. I was so angry and hurt I went downstairs, grabbed a pot, and sticks of butter, boiled it, and went back upstairs into one of the rooms where the boy who raped me stayed, pulled the cover back on my attacker, and poured it on him. You can hear screaming and yelling. Thus, I was beaten by the older boy and others. Staff came running and restrained me and said I was acting out. This would be the first of many times I'll run into Thurston County Olympia, Washington, police for behavioral issues at the Boys Ranch. Rapes, abuse, and violence happened constantly and often, but I kept quiet, silently suffocating, if you will, out of fear of being retaliated by the staff and older boys. Over the course of months in this first year, I started settling down enough to begin taking Ranch trips, and my level started to go up in the ranch level system, so freedom was rewarded a little bit. One of the outings I went on was to a place called "Forbes Lake Kirkland Washington," which was part of the property bought by The Boys Ranch in the 1970s. It was supposed to be a camping trip, but it was not. It was a fucking nightmare shit show for real. I was raped by Matt Zuvich, a staffer newly hired by The Boys Ranch, and I also fought with him on these trips. Plus, I was forced to suck his dick on numerous occasions. It was horrific, to say the least.

..•..

Lake Cushman, Mason, Washington,

4.014.6 Acres and Reservoir.

..•..

It was supposed to be camping trips, therapy sessions, and recreation for the O.K. Boys Ranch. But just like Forbes Lake, it was not. It was a living nightmare. Once again, boys, some of us younger ones, were raped, forced to have group sex, tied up, beaten on, fights broke out, told to be quiet, or punishment would have been measured for being a snitch. I had had enough for me, and by this time, I was super tired of the abuse I received and so severely angered and traumatized that back at the O.K. Boys Ranch, I started to develop a wall against everyone, and I didn't trust shit. A few weeks later, I was at my breaking point. On one occasion, one night, I lost it. I went to the shed on the backyard property, grabbed an axe, and snapped. Running into the Ranch, I started swinging at everything in my line of sight: staff, boys, furniture. I even had the cook, whom I hated so much, backed up by the stove in the kitchen, terrified because she thought I would kill her. I even split the pool table. Somehow, the staff distracted me, knocked the axe out of my hands, restrained me against the wall, their favorite tactic, and called the police again. I fought them, too. They dragged me to the car. It took a couple of officers, and they beat me, slammed my ankle between the car door, restrained me, and pepper sprayed me. Mind you, I was 11 years old going on 12 years old, and these mother fucking raggedy-ass police tortured me as well. So, I was hauled off to the juvenile detention center in Thurston County, Washington. The next day, I went before a judge, caught a record for the incident at the Ranch, and did a little time at the Juvenile Detention Center, Thurston County, Washington. After a month, I returned to the O.K. Boys Ranch.

Over time, things changed. New boys came in, old ones left, violence, rape, strange shit continued. On-call staff changed, resident staff remained, and by this time, as my levels at the Ranch fluctuated, I was placed outside the O.K. Boys Ranch for weekend visits with other families. So, weekend visits started when my levels were good, and when I was bad, and my levels were down, they still sent me, and I think the shit was on purpose because the staff hated me. They sent me to a single male pedophile foster parent who raped and tortured me physically and psychologically. By this time, I was so messed up in the head that I didn't see any relief. On one particular day and weekend, a lady came, and I can't recall her name and her children, but I started seeing her on the weekends and then daily.

I thought this was my way out of this nightmare. She lived on a farm with cows, bulls, chickens, horses, and dogs. And for the first time, I felt a sense of peace and freedom, not scared, and didn't have to worry about sexual and emotional abuse. She, me, and her children became really close, and she wanted to adopt me, and it was in the planning stages. But one day, I got angry and got in trouble at school. I was picked on and started acting out. The ranch staff stopped the visitations with the lady. So much so that Director Thomas van Woerdan told the woman she couldn't adopt me, that I needed to be with a black family only, and so that ended that, the only peace and comfort I had ever known. To this day, I feel like the director had it out for me; he didn't like or care for me. I was like common household trash that you throw away daily. He often punished me; I was utterly devastated.

But eventually, after two years and some months, I was let go. To this day, I feel like they still have a hold on me because they assigned me a caseworker with the DSHS Department of Social Health Services, who was also being paid for services by the O.K. Boys Ranch to monitor and look after me. A harsh reality, these motherfuckers, this O.K. Boys Ranch, had me like a dog, and they were the leash who kept a hold on me. In my eyes, I was never free. I was still a trafficked slave to the system. And so, with that, I was placed with an older woman, a senior citizen, if you will, Mary Jenkins. It was okay; she was an older lady who disappointed me with switches and belts every time I got into trouble, and I would constantly see the Ranch DSHS caseworker. At this time, I was almost out of Middle School, the middle 1980s. I have so many behavioral issues, anger, a wall built up, nightmares of being severely abused, that Mary Jenkins couldn't deal with as an older woman. And she and her oldest daughter decided to have me removed from the home. After a week or so, the caseworker made some calls and found a new home.

James and Gloretta Hoover, new foster parents, North Thurston High School, and the end of my time in the foster care system, mid to late 1980s-1990. I graduated from Nisqually Middle School, Lacey, Washington, and moved with my new foster parents, James and Gloretta Hoover. Gloretta Hoover was a stay-at-home mom with one son, who was kind and sweet. James Hoover was a retired veteran, a strict father, and a security guard for formally Purdy Prison, now called Washington Corrections Center for Women in Harbor, Washington, 98332. This, too, was okay for a while. I started High School at North Thurston High School, Lacey, Washington, 600 Sleater Kinny Road Northeast, a suburb of Olympia, Washington. I was around 14 at the time. I went through the typical high school years. Most of it spent in the special needs section of the high school or special education program. I have many learning and behavioral issues, plus being a rape victim. You develop a lot of crazy shit, but no one knew the rape shit or what I endured at The Boys Ranch out of retaliation that the Boys Ranch would come for me, so I kept quiet. I didn't even trust the Ranch DSHS caseworker with anything. So, I went through my freshman year of high school and was okay. Sophomore year, once again okay, onto my junior year of high school. It was at this time that I had crushes on girls. I learned how to write poetry, got my heart broken, was sad, and got into sports, track and field, my favorite sport. And life seemed okay for a while, but my youthful, painful childhood would again rear its ugly head. And once again, I would get into trouble at school and face my strict foster dad. He beat the shit out of me and placed me outside in the backyard to cut wood all day till I was exhausted, tired, and drained. Gloretta, his wife, always tried talking to me to stay out of trouble. I think she was afraid of him as well because he was one means sonofabitch. He had that security guard, old military-type attitude. I felt that deep one day when I had one of my anger issues at school and had one of my not going to do shit in class; my teacher said something unkind to me, so I grabbed a pencil, sharpened the pencil, thus putting the pencil to the teacher's neck and threatened to kill him. The school and the police said I was acting out, and I took a teacher hostage. They arrested, handcuffed, and hauled me to the Juvenile Detention Center in Thurston County, Washington. I was fingerprinted, booked, and sentenced by a Juvenile Court Thurston County Washington judge the next day and placed in the Juvenile Detention Center Thurston County, Washington, 3000 Pacific Avenue Southeast, Olympia, Washington, 98401. My foster parents were mad, more James than Gloretta Hoover. James said I was a thug and didn't want me back in his home, but Gloretta felt different. Overall, I did a couple of months at the Juvenile Detention Center. For someone going through all this hell I had endured in my life, I should have hated this place. Being locked up and going by rules, I thrived and was content.

After talking to the caseworker, the Hoovers, and the judge, I was ultimately placed back in Hoover's home, even though James didn't like it. I would come to regret that decision to go back later. And so I made it to my senior year of high school and met a nice girl. I went through appendicitis, almost died, and was turning 18. I did well enough to get out of special ed.

Regarding the appendicitis, I had acute appendicitis, and my foster mom, Gloretta, didn't want to take me to the hospital. She tended to her fireplace, gave me medicine, and said sleeping it off would be okay. My foster dad, James Hoover, had a late shift at the prison so he couldn't take me to the hospital. So, I kept on complaining, and finally, she took me. By then, I couldn't walk or use the bathroom, and I collapsed in the emergency room and blacked out. They examined me, took blood work, and, after a few hours, told her that they were glad she brought me in. According to the doctor, my appendix was about to burst. By this time, I was in emergency surgery for a couple of hours, suffering complications because it was difficult to find my appendix. They had to move stuff around and then put it back once it was found and removed. I survived but could have died if I had not been taken to the hospital that night. I was stitched up and then spent a few days in the hospital. After that, I was sent home. My foster dad didn't care what happened to me. He only thought I was trouble. I returned to school, stitched up in pain, but I didn't want to stay home. A month in, and I got in trouble again. And they suspended me from school for a week, which would end my time at the Hoovers. Me and James Hoover got into it and had some words. He told me to go outside in the backyard and cut wood all day. I told him, "Hell no. I'm not going to do it. Fuck that, you do it." James said, "What you say, little nigger?" I said, "Hell no, I'm not going to do it." He snapped, slammed my head against the wall, picked me up, threw me against the wall, then the refrigerator, and choked me badly. I was about to lose consciousness. It took Mrs. Hoover to jump in and get him off me. I truly believe he was going to kill me that day because he hated me so badly. I grabbed whatever I could from my room and ran away, ending up at my friend from the schoolhouse; his parents said I could stay there. They called the police after I explained what happened to my friend's parents. I was sore and bruised, my hand sprained, my back hurt, and I had handprints around my neck where he was trying to choke the life out of me. My spirit was finally broken even more.

The police took statements and pictures and went to my foster parents' home. They talk to Gloretta Hoover first. She told them what her husband did to me, and then they went to talk to James Hoover, who explained what he did. Police told him you're under arrest; place your hands behind your back, read his rights, handcuffed him, and charged him with assault and battery, and he was hauled off to the Thurston County Jail. They told Gloretta I wasn't coming back, as I was 18. I was considered an adult and could make my own decisions. She would have to take it up with O.K. Boys Ranch and the caseworker assigned to my case. So, I stayed with my friends for a while up to 19 years old.

When I turned 19, I got a visit from the O.K. Boys Ranch caseworker. This is around 1990 or so. The caseworker gave me two choices: remain in the foster care system or be permanently released as I was 19 years old, an adult, and could make my own decisions. So, I chose to be released. I signed a pile of paperwork, which released me and freed me from the State of Washington, the foster care system, O. K. Boys Ranch, and the caseworker. I was scared and terrified; what do I do next? I decided to find family and thanked my friend and his family for letting me stay all that time. They said I could have stayed permanently but left Olympia, Washington, in search of family, not looking back. It would be a hard road to find freedom after so many years.

The State of Washington and my handlers failed me. I was a slave, trafficked, sold, sexed by predators numerous times, abused, tortured, and after all these years, finally free.

..●..

Growing Up Fast

- 1990s -

..●..

One of the hardest life lessons is Letting Go and moving on. Whether it's guilt, love, anger, loss, rape, abuse, torture, betrayal, lied on, profiled, or being hurt, no matter what it is in life, change is never easy. We fight to hold on, and we fight to let go. The devil still has a choke hold on my life because I still can't let go of what was done to me, what was out of my control that was sacrificed, my childhood. I just haven't let go.

And so, at the time, I was 19 years old, broken, scarred, damaged, and confused. After being freshly released from the foster care system, I was trying to figure things out. Eight of those years were spent in Olympia, Washington. I spent over a decade in the foster care system and being a slave to the State of Washington. Sixty-five plus foster homes, a few receiving homes, several group homes, and a couple of mental institutions, this was my life. It took a toll on me. It seriously did, and I'm still recovering to this day. Because I was a trafficked slave to the system, it broke me deep. Emotionally, physically, sexually, and mentally killed everything in my life. I didn't even get to graduate from high school. That was very devastating to me. After I signed my release papers, my caseworker gave me bus fare, and we said our goodbyes. I would have to grow up fast on my own now, for the first time in many years, 19 years old, a young adult, in the 1990s, 91 or 92.

I got on the Greyhound bus and went to Pierce County, Tacoma, Washington, searching for family. It was an overwhelming experience for me and a culture shock. Because I was raised white, I acted White. I only listened to White Rock music. Tacoma, Washington, was a mixture of everything that overloaded my senses. I had talked with my grandparents months before while still in the foster care system, who said my mom lives somewhere in Tacoma, Washington. I ended up there and then somehow ended up in Lakewood, Washington, outside in a small suburb neighborhood called Tillicum. I ask around; this is a military-type neighborhood with many people. It led me to a small Chinese store, where the owner said he knew my mom. She lived some ways up the street. I thanked him and made my way there. I knocked on every apartment door till I got to the last door. When that door opened, my mom was standing there. I remember it was tough for me because, at that time, I hadn't seen my mom in several years. The last time I saw my mom, I was a child in the horrific Washington State foster care system, and it was only briefly. So, this was, at this moment, very deep for me. She let me in, which will prove to be a tough life. My mom didn't live in a regular apartment per se, but what they call a studio. A big box to me. You open the door, and the kitchen is right there: a tiny bedroom with no door and a small bathroom. My mom, Ruby, her boyfriend Tommy, and my three brothers I haven't seen in years, Freddy, J.J., and Anthony. My sister, Ramona, didn't live there. She was off running around with different people at that time. But we all lived there, and it proved to be very toxic and challenging, to say the least. I learned how to be black in that environment quickly. And my anger and behavioral issues started to manifest itself once again. On occasion, I got into it with my mom, arguing and fighting with my brothers, and then one day, a big blow-up happened. My mom's boyfriend, Tommy, was abusing my mom and arguing with my mom, so I jumped him, and we fought to the blood. Instead of thanking me for helping her, she hated me for it, and once again, I had to leave. It seemed like throughout my life, shit happens, and I always end up having to leave. This will be a common theme in my life, child life, and adult life. So, I left and stayed at my girlfriend's house, whom I was dating, whom I found on one of those chat lines. I was about 19 years old, early 20's. By then, I was into everything: drugs, random sex with strange women I met on dating sites or phone chat lines. Also, because of my mother, I would experience alcohol again: Everything from malt beverage beer, St Ides, old English 800, any wine, vodka, gin, and my go-to drink at the time called "Cisco," often referred to as liquid crack in my favorite strawberry and orange flavors. Plus, I developed a habit of cigarettes, Newport and Marlboro menthol. Yeah, it was truly a crazy time in my life. And behind my back, my girlfriend was cheating on me with her ex. She was pregnant and claimed it was mine, but it was not. So, once again, I ended up leaving. I met a woman on the dating site and moved to Wichita Falls, Texas, which lasted a few months. Then back to Spokane, Washington, where I met another woman. We ended up lasting a while and eventually moved to Dayton, Texas. We ended up breaking up, her uncle didn't like me, plus I found the whole family freaking strange. They speak in their language, speak in tongues, eat off the land, catch gators and skinned, and eat them. Yeah, Texas was a wild motherfucking place to live in some parts. Finally, one day, my girlfriend's uncle was drinking heavily and said something stupid to me. We exchange words, and he and I get into it. Pushing and shoving, others in the house try to break it up. I try to make my way to our car. He follows me, and before I can close the door, he kicks me in the head and stomach and busts my teeth and lip till I am bleeding everywhere. He threw me out of the house, and I ended up at my girlfriend's cousin's house, where I would stay for a few days. It didn't last long, and I could only call my mom. Mind you, it had been a few months, and my mom had a tiny one-bedroom house now and a new boyfriend named Caesar. They bought me a Greyhound ticket, and I returned to Tacoma, Washington, to live with my mom. This was the middle 1990s, and it wouldn't last for long. When I returned, I also had a new girlfriend, once again messing around with the chat lines. So, one day, me and my girlfriend planned a date. My mom's boyfriend said he'd drive me there and drop me off. Not thinking of anything bad, I said cool, that'd be fine. I told my girlfriend I'd see her soon, and we would have a good night, and she agreed. So, I said goodbye to my mother, and her boyfriend and I took off in the car. Several blocks later, he said he had to make a pit stop, no worries. He had to pick some stuff up from his friend's house. So, when we get there, we stop. I stayed in the car, eager to see my girlfriend, have drinks, and hang out, plus whatever else would come at night when two people were together. Twenty minutes later, my mom's boyfriend Caesar returned to the car, and we took off. We get a few blocks down the street, and suddenly bright lights come on, and all I hear is put your motherfucking hands in the air, don't move, or we will shoot. Caesar stops the car and puts one hand in the air. With the other hand, he is stuffing my pocket with something. He looks at me and tells me no worries, you don't have no record. Just listen to me and tell the police it was your stuff. I was so scared and completely speechless. The police officer said once again, put your motherfucking hands up, and we did as we were told. I was shaking and wondering what the hell was in my pockets because the police were everywhere. They came to the car, put Caesar in one car, then took me to another and placed me up against it. Handcuff me and search my pockets. They also searched the car for guns or any other illegal things. And in my pockets, they pull 20 big crack rocks out. After that, they Read Me My Rights and placed me in the car. An officer comes along, gets in the car, and asks me which drugs are these. I look over, Caesar staring at me from the other police car and shaking his head no. And so I started to remember, as a child, being abused. I learned not to snitch, so I wasn't going to do it now in this case, so I told the police officer the drugs were mine. "Police officer says for drug possession with intent to deliver, I would be facing 5 or 10 years in prison.".

Unknown to me then, my mom's boyfriend was a drug dealer with a very long criminal record with two strikes. I always thought he was a strange man. Well, the police took me off to jail. That was mind-blowing because I had no adult jail record. My juvenile records were sealed years ago. I was booked and fingerprinted at the Pierce County Jail, Tacoma, Washington. I stripped off my clothing, searched, and placed in a holding tank. I was fed a meal and allowed to place one phone call. I called my mom. She said listen to me. She wanted me to take the fall for Caesar because I had no criminal record as an adult, and she thought they were going to be lenient on me, give me probation, and just let me go. This will prove that wasn't the case. After all, this is Washington state, and they screw you if you're black. They throw you in the system and let you rot.

The next day, I went before a judge, pre-arraignment, and a pretrial date was set. My public attorney at the time said good luck, and that was that. So, I was handcuffed once again and taken back to the holding tank. Eventually, after a few days, I made my way to what they call the population. I was moved all over the jail for a few months and suffered there. On one occasion, I got sexually molested in a jail shower, held down by one inmate while another anal penetrated me. It was one of my worst feelings and pain to be violated like that. Still, as a child, I should have been used to it as I was numerously raped over and over again as a child, so being an adult, I should have just shaken it off like many things, but there's a code in jail, and that code is: You don't snitch, snitches get stitches, so I didn't tell. Someone else did. I don't know who because days later, I was taken to a nursing station to be examined and then to the chief sheriff's office, where they interviewed and investigated the situation. But I refused to say anything, and the matter was closed, even though a nurse said something traumatic happened to me. Also, a few weeks later, I almost got stabbed. I was making a phone call, and an inmate wanted me off. I said, "No, I got my allotted time, and I'm not getting off." He got pissed off and tried to stab me with a pencil. At the time, jail guards watched because they were doing inmate counts. An alarm went off, the guy was taken down, tasered, we all got locked in our room, and they took the guy to solitary confinement. I went through a lot of terrible shit in that place and a lot of trauma and abuse emotionally and physically during that time.

Two and a half to three months in, I got a new attorney, not a public defender, but a regular attorney. I was told that sometimes, an attorney would take on cases for free as a public service to the community when he feels that someone is innocent. I can tell you this guy was not ordinary; he was extraordinary. He said he would get me out and read my case file. Something didn't sit well with him. He said he would represent me for free if I told him the truth," I said the truth!!!" he said, "Yes, the truth." The truth is that these were not my drugs. I'm not a drug dealer, don't have an adult record, and shouldn't be in jail. So, I stared at the attorney for a while and said nothing. So once again, my attorney said he could get me out entirely and that we would meet again in a few weeks to strategize and go over my case, and I need to hold on. Now, mind you, the jail code: Don't snitch; snitches get stitches. That was my thought. So, I broke down and told the attorney everything, crying too while speaking. He wrote everything down. After that, he said he would see me in a few weeks, and I did a good job. He also requested that I have a cell by myself and made a note to the chief sheriff.

Until then, I was to be taken back to my cell. I shook my attorney's hand and was handcuffed on the way back to my cell. At this time, I remember I was placed in population, but somehow, it got around that I was a snitch. When we got close to the cell tank, some guy yelled out, that motherfucker right there is a snitch, a rat; we are going to break him off. Caesar happened to be in that cell tank, and he looked at me and told me, you fucked up. Me and your mom were trying to help you, young bro. But you snitch, you're dead to me, and proceeds to yell at the guard, bring that young motherfucker in here.

The guard tells everyone to calm down, or they'd be in trouble, but they got noisier and started throwing all kinds of shit around; the alarm goes off, and guards come running everywhere. The guard holding me explains to the other guards what happened. So, every one of the inmates went to their rooms, and they were locked down. The guard holding me decides to take me to an isolation unit for safety reasons. A report was made and given to the Chief Sheriff, and a copy was forwarded to my attorney. I was truly terrified. Had they put me in that tank with all of them inmates, I would have been raped and murdered for telling my truths. A few weeks later was my hearing. I was placed shackled on my wrists and my ankles. I was led down the hallway with the guard through a locked door and then another door before we got to the courtroom. Another guard comes from another direction with Caesar, my mom's boyfriend. He was also shackled but only on the wrists. He looks at me and says," You didn't have to snitch. Me and your mom were trying to help you." I look at Caesar and say, "Fuck you bitch, you try to use me and exploit me." The guard says, "Shut the hell up and toe the line." Caesar snaps and tries to come for me. Me and him up against the wall, struggling to get at each other. He did manage to get his hands around my neck even though he was handcuffed at the wrists. It turns into chaos. The light and sound go off, and other guards come running. They pry us apart. I'm told to chill out and placed in a holding room before the courtroom. Caesar is going off kicking at guards, and they tackle and tase him, a couple of guards holding him down for safety reasons. He is ultimately dragged back to his cell unit. I hear a door open in the holding room, and my attorney enters. I explained to my attorney what happened. He said that was unfortunate, explaining that they were going to try me and Caesar at the same time. Because this incident in the hallway happened, that would change things, and only I would be going into the courtroom today. He also said I would probably lose if I were to get a trial with Caesar. It pissed me off when this man said he can set me free, but I continue to listen. He told me I would go before a judge today, and I was to play dumb, act like I wasn't listening, and drool at the mouth. I thought this was some strange shit he was telling me, but I continued to listen. He said if I didn't do this, I would have a trial with Caesar, and the outcome wouldn't be in my favor since the drugs were in my pocket. My attorney says, this way, I will get a trial by myself, but I must spend 30 days at Western State Hospital, Steilacoom, Washington, to see if I can stand trial. Washington State Hospital resides in Steilacoom, Washington, on the outskirts of Tacoma, Washington. So, I went into court for my omnibus hearing before a judge, no jury, just my attorney and the state attorneys, and I didn't say shit but did exactly what my attorney told me to do, plus I acted spaced out. Every time the judge said something to me. I went in another direction. And the judge had no choice but to sentence me to 30 days at Western State Hospital. Mind you, Western State Hospital is a mental health hospital, not a regular Hospital. To be evaluated to stand trial. I signed the papers. My attorney said everything would be all right and he would see me in 30 days. He also winked at me and said good job. A few days later, I was called up, placed on a bus, and driven to Western State Hospital. I was nervous but felt relief. After all I went through in jail, emotionally, physically, and sexually molested, this seemed like freedom. I arrived 40 minutes later, uncuffed, and handed over to hospital staff. I walked through a locked door, was taken to a room, and given a t-shirt, sweats, toothbrush, toothpaste, and towels. They took my clothes, and I showered. Once done, I was assigned a room and told to wait there. Someone would be with me shortly. Also, my toothbrush was taken away; this is a mental health hospital, so I understood. An hour later, hospital staff came and took me to the medical office, where I was examined, evaluated, and my blood drawn, then led to the counselor therapist's office. This was the head counselor of the facility. The counselor writes notes on the chart and then tells me the rules and behaviors I must follow. He also explained that this is (RCW 71.05) a civil commitment order by a judge to see if I can stand trial (trial competency evaluation) for 30 days. All of this was explained to me, plus I would see him and an assistant counselor for the 30 days I was there daily. After that, a nurse comes in with a small cup of pills I must take. (Ritalin and some other bullshit). I thought this was strange, and I didn't like it. I thought, "Why would I have to take a pill for an evaluation? " So, I got pissed off, started crying, tried to get up and leave, and refused to take the pills but was forced by the clinic staff. The chief counselor said," If I didn't comply, he would write a bad evaluation, and it wouldn't look good in court, so I calmed down and did as I was told. So, over the next few days, then some weeks, I would go to the daily grind of Western State Hospital life. Only getting in trouble once or twice, placed in a strait jacket once or twice, and placed in isolation rooms. I believe I was getting frustrated and tired of taking all those pills and being doped up on a daily basis. Eventually, I got everything under control enough, and by my 30th day, Pierce County sheriff came and retrieved me, and I was taken back to Pierce County Jail. I refused to go into the population, so they put me in the hole, very tiny jail cells with concrete beds, no blankets, or pillows for a few days; that's where inmates go if they cause trouble in the jail, even though I wasn't in any trouble. After that, I was placed in a single-cell isolation unit. A week or two went by, and my attorney came to see me in one of the council rooms they had at the jail, where I would often meet my attorney. He tells me," It's going to be two separate trials, one for me and one for Caesar, my mom's boyfriend. And there's a plenty good chance I would get off without a record.

I would come to know this as a lie, as often as I was always lied to because Washington State Courts, just like the raggedy-ass foster care system, are designed to stick you, leave you, confuse you, and trap you in the system, especially if you're black. So, my attorney gave me two choices: trial by jury or go before a judge. So, I chose the judge as a better choice. My attorney writes everything down and tells me everything will be all right here on out, no worries, and he sees me at trial. A few weeks went by, mind you. I damn near spent four and a half months locked up, so when the time came, I was relieved to get this over with, no matter my fate. I admit I was scared and nervous. A guard came to my isolation cell unit and led me down the hallway to one unlocked door and another to that same holding room just before the courtroom. After a few minutes, I was there in the courtroom, and there was no one there to support me except my attorney, state attorneys, the jail guidance counselor, who got it approved for me to wear my regular clothes in court, and my brother Anthony who I hadn't seen in years. And I talked to him several times on the phone while incarcerated. He told me what happened as far as Caesar was concerned. My mom didn't come. She didn't want to have anything to do with me because I didn't want to take the fall for her boyfriend, Caesar.

In front of the judge, I was read my rights, and evidence and police reports were presented. Twenty big crack rocks evidence bags were placed on the evidence table. Unknown to me at this time, and my attorney didn't mention it, Caesar already had his trial a month ago, confessed everything, and sentenced him to prison. Remember, he had an extensive criminal record, so he got sentenced for a long time in prison. After some back and forth, plus the state attorney saying they wanted to stick me with more time and arguing with my attorney. The judge threw his gavel between both parties and said, "He has heard enough..."

he also warned both parties, state Attorneys and my attorney to chill out. He got this. He turns to me and says, "Mr. Dumas, this is big evidence here, and I could sentence you to the maximum allowed by Court standards and Washington State Standards, but I'm not going to do that today. Your attorney's reports, the jail guidance counselor's report, Western State Hospital reports, statements from your brother, and your co-defendant's confession, I believe that you were a victim in all this. You were a victim and all this in the wrong place at the wrong time. But to satisfy the court, I'm placing you on two years' probation, ordering you to pay court costs, and have no dealings with Mr. Caesar, is that clear?" mind you, I received a felony, not a misdemeanor, nor clear record like my attorney tried to get for me. So, I told the judge, yes, it's clear. He asked the State prosecutor if there was anything further from the state and anything further from my attorney, and both parties said no. Then the judge turns back to me and says, "With that, this case is dismissed, and good luck, Mr. Dumas, with the rest of your life." I thanked my attorney, hugged him, and I was even allowed to hug my brother. Place back in handcuffs, I was led back to the jail, to my single isolation unit. A week and a half pass, and I'm released from jail. I was assigned a probation officer, and life started again. I had nowhere to go except my girlfriend. I moved with my girlfriend for a while, but she cheated on me and dogged me with one of her exes, and once again, I was on the move.

Two years go by, I'm released from probation, and once again, I find myself back with my mom, briefly, this time. She had another new boyfriend and lived in a one-bedroom studio apartment in Lakewood, Washington, in a ghetto part of town called "Chocolate City." I would stay there for several months and then move on. In 1997, I briefly went to jail for the destruction of property. Also, in 1997, I would become homeless once again. In late 1997, I used the chat line again and met a woman I would eventually fall in love with. This would be my first time falling in love with anybody. And I thought this was it, I'd finally found peace, so I thought, a life, a family. This woman, Michelle Ray, gave me hope and a future. By June 1998, we were married. I was somewhere in my twenties, and she was 31 years old. I always thirsted for older women, and I don't know why. Young women don't do it for me. But like everything in my life, this too would come to pass. My marriage and friendship to this beautiful woman did not end on a sour note. I was young, and I wasn't ready to handle being with a mature woman, nor handle life after all that was done to me for so many years. The day I left, I was heartbroken; I cried. I was miserable and sick inside, but I packed my bags, said my goodbyes, and moved on again. And I would end up with this person, that person, suffering homelessness and starvation once again, and really go through it at that time.

By 1999, I returned to my mom again and then moved on. I met a woman in Portland, Oregon, who would become the mother of my fraternal twins, Malik and Nazari. I later took a paternity test and never met them. They are now 23 years old as of February 2023. In 1999, that was a toxic time and toxic situation. It would only last a month and a half that I was there, and once again, I would move on. By this time, I had moved on so often and gone through so much hell and shit in my life, emotionally, physically, and sexually. I was completely broken up and fucked up in my head and life. By the end of 1999, I was severely homeless until the year 2000 and beyond, where new chapters of my life, sad, hopeless, broken, abusive fucked up chapters of my life, would begin.

·•·•·

The Next Chapter of My Life...

Silently Suffering

Hoping for a Future

·•·•·

All I've been through, all that I endured, the trauma, the pain, the rapes, lies and betrayal of my life. I'm one emotionally angry, broken man. A lesser man would have fallen apart, gave up, and died. I'm still here, suffering and speaking my truth. To those who don't understand, let my suffering speak to you directly, understanding who " Walter Dumas» is and why I›m silently suffocating.

Forty-plus years of abuse, torture, and sexually preyed upon, destroying my youthful innocence and partially my adult life, breaking me emotionally. Leaving me with heaviness, uneasiness, unbearable, heartbreaking life journey. Enduring, suffering silently, my life crashing daily, like a sinking ship on an ocean, this is my life. A life that, for years, I felt my hope impossible, my faith non-existent, just darkness and fears consuming and deeply overwhelming me. Mourning, unhappy, sad, grieving, distressed, this is all in one part of my life, which gave me post-traumatic stress, insomnia, and other things so unpleasant. It's why I don't trust people too well. I don't care for friendships, no joy, happiness, or peace. And relationships with women, no pleasure, no ecstasy, no sex. Just me surviving alone, my heart gently weeping, tormented, dejected, is how I cope with life. And I'm so tired and exhausted from all this, and why I feel like if death came to my door, I would welcome it with open arms. Like death suffocated my life and let me close my eyes and rest forever.

"Hope and A Future ..."

And even though I feel all this and I'm suffering, I feel that to have hope and a future, you must go through something in life because life ain't easy, nor is it perfect. Trials, obstacles, and hardships will come your way whether you like it or not; it's a given, automatic, and human nature. So, I'm going through all this deep sadness and pain, but have faith enough to know to hold on. God will provide, and God will give me hope and a future...

(Jeremiah 29:11 King James Version)

Says : "For I know the plans I have for you, declares the Lord, plans to prosper you and not harm you, to give you Hope and a future."

And so I take this Bible verse, and I Hold On, knowing that if I find something to guide me and direct me from all this hurt, trauma, and pain, life Will Go On. So, I keep this in my heart and mind cuz I got so much going on in my life, that one day I will be made whole and set free. I must keep working at getting there.

And to let people know, you just can't drop, sweep under the rug, or let go of 40 years plus years of abuse, I'm a broken work in progress, and so when people get like that, I think they're hypocrites, cuz they're trying to be perfect like they got it all going on but every human got something hidden if you will " skeletons in the closet," I don't give a damn Who You Are, including me. So, I'm not happy nor perfect I'm scarred, like I say, broken, damaged goods, but at least I'm not hiding it, for there's purpose and direction telling my truths, my story, and my goals of healing, recovery, hope, and a future. And so, I will get there one day. It's only a matter of time.

"Quote- " *The road may not be smooth, but the Journey is worth the ride."*

After going through so much in my life, finding myself is a long journey, so I'm allowing myself the grace to find the meaning in every phase of a purposeful life, along the way enduring setbacks and hardships. And going through all this with confidence and knowing that all will be as it's meant to be because I have faith in God and accept, what I been through with sacrifice. Knowing my faith in God has given me the strength of a lion. Understanding the road may not be smooth, but the journey is worth the ride.

·· ● ··

Being An Adult

After a Traumatic Childhood...

·· ● ··

A lot of my days, I sit alone in a dark bathroom and just cry it out. My breathing shallow, my heart in deep pain, suffering in silence. It is because I'm dealing with so many things. Physical, emotional, and mental. There's no smile, there's no laughter; my sadness is a mask that I wear well. Understand I had to grow up into adulthood carrying so much baggage from a traumatic childhood. One that haunts me even now at 50 years old. How I'm able to work every day, take care of a wife who's disabled, and just be myself on top of dealing with my disease, which is called trauma, I'm just not going to lie to you; it's really mother fucking hard, it truly is. My life is just full of twists and turns, brutal at times, to say the least. Suffering and suffocated often, how I'm standing and moving forward is a chapter in a book of my life that is still being written. How it all ends, I just don't know, when the trauma Predator is still present in my life, that weighs me down like a boat anchor. I tried everything to be free from a psychotherapist at Seamar Behavioral Health in Tacoma, Washington, for a few months to a year, but they weren't there to take care of me or to help me like they were supposed to. They just write shit down and then prescribe you all kinds of medications that didn't help me. It ruined my life as well. They were the O.K. Boys Ranch of my adult life... Giving me seven different medications at the same time, just doping me up: Risperdal, Lexapro, Ritalin, Wellbutrin, Clonazepam, Lorazepam, and Ziprasidone (Geodon) just to name a few. Drugs didn't help me; it was the total opposite. This shit, that was supposed to make me anti-depressant, anti-anxiety, anti-psychotic, did the total opposite, it made me a drug addict, and the side effects from all this shit they gave me ,made me mad, anger, drowsy, dizzy, irregular heartbeat, muscle spasms, weight gain, restlessness and suicidal...I remember one day coming to my therapist office, I just had enough, I took all seven medications, and drunk a couple bottles of alcohol, I was high as a kite, but I also felt like I was dying. So, I remember getting to the therapist office, waiting for my appointment, when it came, I went into her office and sat in a chair, my breathing was very heavy, sweating out of control. My therapist asked me was I okay, but I wasn't, all I remember is her yelling for her secretary. Everything went dark after that. I was in darkness for a very long time, till this day I really truly believe I had died in that therapeutic office. When I woke up, I was in the hospital. From what I was told, it seems like I was gone, and they filled my body with some black substance, to reverse the effects of a severe overdose. They asked me was I trying to kill myself, I said no, because I knew If I said yes, they probably would have sent me to Washington State Hospital. So, I stayed in the hospital there, St Joseph's Hospital in Tacoma, Washington for a couple days. I talked to a counselor there, signed the paperwork, and hours later released. Like I said many things I have tried to cope, alcohol various times, chain smoking cigarettes, experimented with drugs and random sex with different women. I think I did that last part just to try and escape all the rape and abuse I endured, but to no avail. I am just living and silently suffocating, and it hurts so damn bad. The monster is my trauma, and it affects me on a daily basis. Every day is different, I may smile on some days, but it's not real it's just a mask to cover up the real truths and keep people from questioning, and on other days I am one pissed off angry man. But that's how I function in my life, and I hate people who tell me to suck it up, forget about it and Let It Go. These motherfuckers, haven't lived what I've been through, walked a mile in my shoes, seen the horrors of abuse and gone through that abuse that was inflicted on me. Some of these people are weak and wouldn't have survived what I went through, experienced on numerous occasions, endured, and suffered. And so, these are people I try to stay away from because they don't understand all that has destroyed my life. As I write this, I'm rebuilding my life, it's not easy, it's challenging, it's difficult. It's been a long road and I'm still traveling on that road, to find comfort, joy, peace, happiness, and meaningful relationships. Also, trusting people because I've been exploited so much, you just don't know who to trust. So, until I find that, I'm just silently suffocating, trying to hold on.

··•··

Thoughts, Feelings, and Emotions Moving Forward...

"Trauma."

··•··

"Trauma is the predatorial fear that Creeps in your life on a daily basis, that interrupts your life, sometimes destroys your life, and keeps you awake every night; that's trauma to me ..."

.... Living a traumatic, broken life is the hardest thing to do every day, but I live this life every day. Monday through Sunday, seven days a week. I am truly lucky to even be alive, after all the traumatic experiences, from childhood to adulthood. I should have been dead a long time ago, I would have been at peace with it. Most people don't understand when I say that, but it's how I live my life daily...

... And as I live this traumatic life and tell my story, it's not for the faint of heart, unless you lived it, experienced it, and went through it as I have. Trauma is my disease; I've lived with it for 40-plus years. It was a disaster, it was violent, it was Criminal, I lost my soul and spirit, my childhood, some parts of my adulthood, it was hurtful, painful, abusive, physical, and molested sexually on numerous occasions. You can say most of the shit that happened in my life was catastrophic. This is what shaped my life. It made me feel bad, scared, hurt and ashamed of me and made me feel less than, like I often say, like trash. I still haven't made sense of the entire complexity of what my life is now, no matter if I am man or woman, gay or straight, this or they, him or her, alien, fuck I don't know. And no matter how often I try to tell myself, the past is the past or to write it off, that trauma on a daily, reminds me, triggers me, and rears its ugly head. So, if I was to be honest with my damn self, I'm still stuck in my pain, abuse, and torture... So, understand, trauma is my cancer with no cure.

It is Fentanyl that knocks me out unconscious. This trauma has affected my marriage, family, friends, my social life even though I don't have one, and makes me disassociate. This trauma also caused me to have a jail record and other things that are not good in my life. So that's why I often say, "fuck life," because some days, my life might be okay, good if it makes any sense, and then other days, it can be a complete and total fucking mess. My life is a real-life circus, a true shit show, and I am the ringmaster with Predators lurking...And so, one day, I'm going to have to get a narrative to move on in life, but it is not now. I'm still dealing with life, like a card player at a bad poker tournament. My Traumatized Life Is the Beast That Haunts Me Day In And Day Out. This Is Trauma, My Trauma.

WALTER DUMAS

Milton Keynes UK
Ingram Content Group UK Ltd.
UKHW052359160224
437951UK00014B/635

9 780982 876886